BEHIND THE WHEEL™

Matt Kenseth

NASCAR Driver

Jeffrey Spaulding

rosen publishing's
rosen central®

New York

For Sally Ganchy—thank you for making me laugh

Published in 2009 by The Rosen Publishing Group, Inc.
29 East 21st Street, New York, NY 10010

Library of Congress Cataloging-in-Publication Data

Spaulding, Jeffrey, 1934–
Matt Kenseth: NASCAR driver / Jeffrey Spaulding.—1st ed.
    p. cm.—(Behind the wheel)
Includes bibliographical references and index.
ISBN-13: 978-1-4042-1897-0 (library binding)
ISBN-13: 978-1-4358-5404-8 (pbk)
ISBN-13: 978-1-4358-5410-9 (6 pack)
1. Kenseth, Matt. 2. Automobile racing drivers—United States—
Biography. 3. NASCAR (Association) 4. Stock car racing—United
States. I. Title.
GV1032.K455S63 2009
796.72092—dc22
[B]
                                                           2008029063

Manufactured in the United States of America

On the cover: Matt Kenseth sits behind the wheel of his #17 DeWalt Ford during practice for the NASCAR Sprint Cup Series Kobalt Tools 500 at the Atlanta Motor Speedway in Hampton, Georgia.

CONTENTS

Introduction 4

Chapter **1** The Early Years 8

Chapter **2** The Big Time 14

Chapter **3** A Taste of Victory 23

Chapter **4** The Road Ahead 33

Glossary 41

For More Information 42

For Further Reading 44

Bibliography 45

Index 47

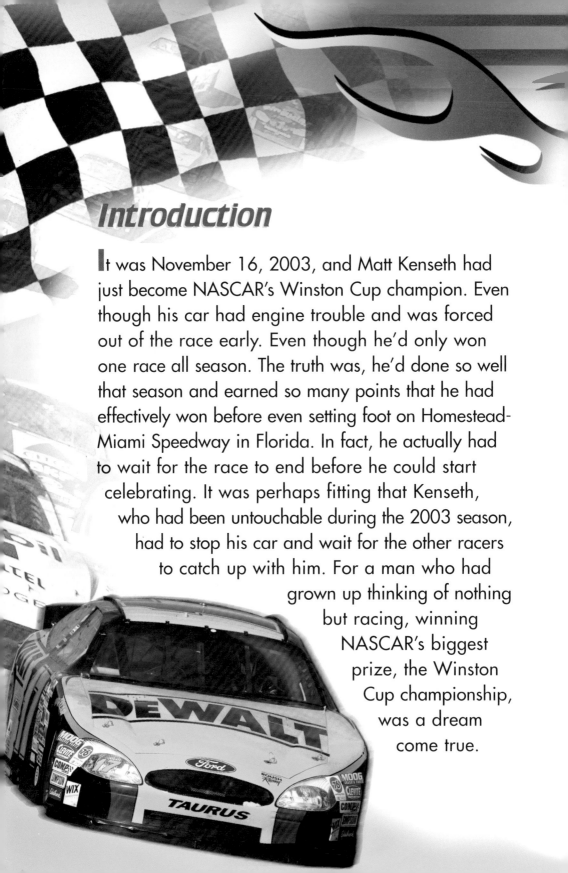

Introduction

It was November 16, 2003, and Matt Kenseth had just become NASCAR's Winston Cup champion. Even though his car had engine trouble and was forced out of the race early. Even though he'd only won one race all season. The truth was, he'd done so well that season and earned so many points that he had effectively won before even setting foot on Homestead-Miami Speedway in Florida. In fact, he actually had to wait for the race to end before he could start celebrating. It was perhaps fitting that Kenseth, who had been untouchable during the 2003 season, had to stop his car and wait for the other racers to catch up with him. For a man who had grown up thinking of nothing but racing, winning NASCAR's biggest prize, the Winston Cup championship, was a dream come true.

Surrounded by his crew members, Matt Kenseth and his wife, Katie, smile for the cameras. Kenseth is holding the Winston Cup trophy after winning the 2003 championship.

Kenseth is part of NASCAR's next generation, a group of young racers redefining the sport of stock car racing. Unlike many older NASCAR racers, who traditionally have Southern roots, Kenseth comes from the state of Wisconsin, way up north near the Great Lakes. In stock car racing's early years, many racers were hot-tempered, rough-and-tumble, flashy "good ol' boys." Kenseth, in contrast, has always been extremely mature

5

and even-tempered. He is generally considered a consummate professional. In many ways, Kenseth is an example of how much stock car racing has grown and how far it has come from its humble roots.

The National Association of Stock Car Auto Racing (NASCAR) was officially established in 1948, when Bill France decided to formally organize the ragtag gang of daredevils involved in early stock car racing. The roots of the sport, however, can be traced back to 1920, when the 18th Amendment was added to the Constitution of the United States. The 18th Amendment effectively prohibited the sale of alcohol. This law, known as Prohibition, did not eliminate the demand for alcohol, however. Homemade liquor, known as moonshine, was produced and distributed all over the country. Besides being sometimes poisonous, moonshine—and the production, selling, and drinking of it—was illegal.

The men who transported moonshine, sometimes known as "whiskey trippers," often modified their cars so as to be able to better outrun the police. When Prohibition ended in 1933, these drivers suddenly found themselves out of a job. Accustomed to driving fast, taking risks, and outpacing other drivers for a living, the former whiskey trippers began racing each other for fun.

Stock car racing was different from other kinds of racing, such as Indy Car and Formula One, because the cars being raced were almost the same as the street cars that were driven by normal, everyday people (in this context, the term "stock" means unmodified). NASCAR was established as a sanctioning body, or an organization that institutes rules to ensure fair competition and safety. As NASCAR racing grew, the cars themselves began to change. Modern stock cars are completely customized, resembling street cars in body shape only. And today's stock car drivers are trained athletes, not hard-driving criminals on the fringes of society. NASCAR has grown away from its somewhat unsavory past to become one of the most popular sports in the United States.

Matt Kenseth exemplifies the new breed of NASCAR driver. He is polite and professional, unassuming, and 100 percent devoted to racing. From his humble beginnings in small-town Wisconsin to his current fame and fortune, Kenseth has exemplified what it means to be a true champion.

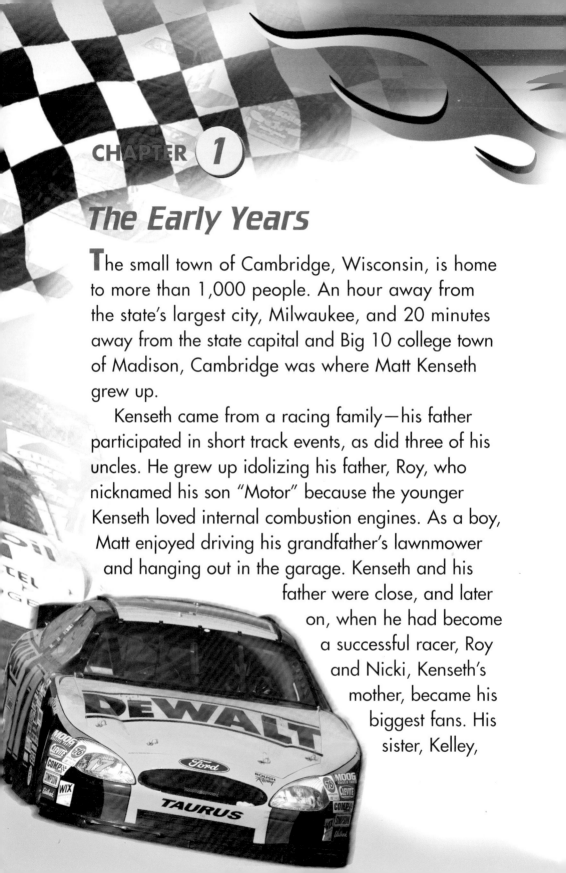

CHAPTER 1

The Early Years

The small town of Cambridge, Wisconsin, is home to more than 1,000 people. An hour away from the state's largest city, Milwaukee, and 20 minutes away from the state capital and Big 10 college town of Madison, Cambridge was where Matt Kenseth grew up.

Kenseth came from a racing family—his father participated in short track events, as did three of his uncles. He grew up idolizing his father, Roy, who nicknamed his son "Motor" because the younger Kenseth loved internal combustion engines. As a boy, Matt enjoyed driving his grandfather's lawnmower and hanging out in the garage. Kenseth and his father were close, and later on, when he had become a successful racer, Roy and Nicki, Kenseth's mother, became his biggest fans. His sister, Kelley, gave him his first car: a 1982 Honda Accord. It was hardly the sort of car that you would see on a racetrack, but for a kid who liked anything with an engine and four wheels, it was a special gift.

Kenseth acquired his first race car through a special arrangement with his father. Roy agreed to purchase a race car for his son. Roy would drive the car until Matt was old enough to take it over. In the meantime, the younger Kenseth would work on the car for his dad. That way, he could learn all about what went into maintaining a good race car. Kenseth was only 13 years old when his father bought the car, meaning he would have to wait three long years before he could drive it himself.

Starting Out

Kenseth started racing when he was 16. But he didn't start out racing in NASCAR—not by a long shot. Across the USA, there are many small, local racing series that serve as stepping-stones to NASCAR's Cup Series. All stock drivers participate in these smaller series. There, they gain valuable experience and, hopefully, find the sponsors that will fund their burgeoning racing careers. In 1988, Kenseth began racing at nearby Wisconsin tracks such as the Columbus 151 Speedway (where his very first race took place) and the Jefferson Speedway. His family wasn't wealthy, but their support meant the world to

Kenseth is a hero among racing fans in his home state. Here, he waves to his admirers before the Miller Lite Nationals at Slinger Speedway in Slinger, Wisconsin.

him. His grandfather Helmer was always willing to lend his grandson a hand, even buying tires if Matt needed them.

From the beginning, it was apparent that Kenseth had a lot of potential. He even won his third feature event! It wasn't long before he started racing at Madison International Speedway and Slinger Speedway. At these tracks, he participated in late-model events, one of the highest classes of stock car racing outside of professional tracks. By the time he was 19 years old, Kenseth was in the thick of competitive racing.

Many observers were impressed with his skill and mature approach to racing. His growing number of wins, titles, and championships in various racing series in Wisconsin, such as a 1994 win in the Slinger Nationals, garnered a lot of attention for the young amateur. But in 1995, he really began making a mark on the racing world. He did well in the All-Pro Series, winning one-quarter of all the races for the season. Clearly, this mild-mannered Wisconsinite meant business. The next year, he did well in the USAR Hooters Series and made his first appearance in NASCAR's Busch Series (now known as the Nationwide Series).

Joining the Busch Series

The Busch Series is not the most prestigious NASCAR racing series. Rather, it is a place where promising stock car racers hone their skills and prepare for the ultimate in stock car racing competition, NASCAR's "big leagues," the Cup Series. Sometimes, drivers who regularly compete in the Cup Series will race in the Busch Series, but it is generally considered a proving ground for less experienced racers. Busch Series cars are slightly different than those run in the Cup Series, and drivers who do well often get a chance to move up and race in the big time. In the Busch Series, Kenseth would be racing against some of the greatest stock car drivers in the United States and, by extension, the entire world. Kenseth's first Busch Series race took place in May 1996 at the 1.5-mile (2.4 kilometer) Lowe's Motor Speedway in Concord, North Carolina.

In 1997, he had a successful run in the important American Speed Association (ASA) Series, a late-model car racing association. He was running an impressive second in points when he got the phone call that would launch his NASCAR racing career. The man on the other end of the line was Robbie Reiser, a former competitor of Kenseth's who was fielding his own Busch Series team. It seems that one of Reiser's drivers, a fellow named Tim Bender, had sustained an injury that was keeping him away from the track. Reiser needed a competent driver to fill in for Bender. Having driven against Kenseth, Reiser thought that he would be a good substitute driver.

Initially, Kenseth was only slated to cover for Bender for six races. But the plan changed after he ran the first two races—he placed 11th in the first, and a remarkable seventh in the second. Reiser was pleasantly surprised that the replacement driver had no problem racing on longer tracks. In fact, Reiser was so impressed that he had the 25-year-old stay for the rest of the season.

It soon became clear that Reiser made the right decision. Behind the wheel of the #17 car, Kenseth ran 21 of 30 races in 1997. While he didn't score any wins, he placed in the top five twice and in the top ten seven times, finishing out the year in 22nd place. It was a respectable placing, all things considered. The following year, however, his performance was more than just respectable—it was awe-inspiring.

In 1998, the 26-year-old wunderkind competed in all 31 of the season's Busch Series races, garnering three wins, 17 top fives, and an astounding 23 top tens. Kenseth earned close to a million dollars that year and finished second in the Busch Series points standings behind Dale Earnhardt Jr., heir to the Earnhardt racing dynasty. As was the case with Kenseth, Earnhardt Jr.'s father had helped him get a start in racing. However, unlike Kenseth's case, Earnhardt Jr.'s father, the uncompromising Dale Earnhardt Sr., also known as "the Intimidator," was one of the greatest stock car drivers that the world has ever known. Although Dale Jr. didn't drive with his father's furious abandon, he was still a formidable opponent—an opponent that Kenseth would end up racing against for much of his professional career.

CHAPTER 2

The Big Time

The most important racing series in NASCAR is the Sprint Cup Series (sometimes simply referred to as "the Cup Series"). The series was originally known as the Strictly Stock Series, and then the Grand National Series. Later, it was sponsored by Winston and was therefore renamed the Winston Cup. For a short time, with sponsor Nextel, it became the Nextel Cup. Today, it is called the Sprint Cup. Sprint Cup drivers compete against the best stock car racers in the United States, if not the world. They win huge cash prizes, score lucrative sponsorship deals, and can become international celebrities. In garages and short tracks all over the United States, hopeful young stock car drivers dream of racing in the Cup Series. Matt Kenseth was no exception.

Bill Elliott *(right)* is a
NASCAR legend. Kenseth
filled in for Elliott in a
Winston Cup Series race
when the older driver's
father died.

Called Up to the Cup Series

In 1998, veteran NASCAR
driver Bill Elliott, who had won the
Winston Cup championship a decade before, was forced
to bow out of a race. Many drivers will try to compete in
a race no matter what, even if it means just making one
lap around the track before quitting, because even a
last-place finish means that they will win a couple of points.
However, Elliott wasn't injured. Instead, he had suffered
a personal tragedy: his father had died, and he was
going to the funeral. Kenseth was called up to fill in for
Elliott, driving the #94 car for 400 laps at Dover Raceway
in Delaware.

It was the first time that Kenseth would be driving
against a Cup Series field composed of 42 of the greatest

stock car drivers in the world. He surprised everyone that day by finishing sixth—only one place away from the top five. Although he didn't lead any laps, the young firebrand came away with 150 points.

Winning Points

At the heart of NASCAR racing is the points system. For every race that a driver competes in, he or she earns points. When drivers break the NASCAR rules, they may lose points from their season total. Until recently, the rules were simple: the driver with the most points at the end of the season won NASCAR's championship. Finishing first in a race earns a driver a whopping 180 points. A second place finish results in 170 points. Beyond second place, each successive finish is worth five fewer points. For instance, a third place finish nets a driver 165 points; a fourth place finish, 160 points. The point increment drops to four for drivers who finished in seventh to 11th place, and then to three points beyond that. Five extra points can be acquired by leading a lap, and another five for leading the most laps of any driver racing that day.

A hallmark of Kenseth's driving style is that he forgoes taking risks to concentrate on racking up points. Out of all the NASCAR racers, he has one of the lowest incidences of collisions and crashes. While other drivers might bump a car they are following to pass it, Kenseth generally prefers to sit back and wait for an opportunity to make a

Behind the wheel of the distinctive #17 DeWalt car, Matt Kenseth runs a Busch Series prequalifying heat at Daytona International Speedway.

clean pass. He is content to finish second or third, rather than win a race, and still collect a large number of points toward his season total.

Kenseth continued to hone his point-focused driving technique in the Busch Series in 1999, where he was trying to top his 1998 performance and win the championship. The Kenseth-Reiser partnership proved to be fruitful once again, and Kenseth got a new sponsor in the form of DeWalt Tools. Together, Kenseth, Reiser, and DeWalt won four Busch Series races, placing in the top five 14 times and the top ten 20 times. Overall, Kenseth finished third in the Busch Series points standing, behind Jeff Green and Dale Earnhardt Jr., who took the Busch championship for the second year in a row.

Successful Substitute Driving

Kenseth's success substituting for Bill Elliott led to more opportunities to race as a replacement driver in the Winston Cup Series. In March 1999, at Darlington Raceway in South Carolina, the car driven by Bobby Labonte skidded into a wall after hitting a patch of fluid on the track during a prerace practice lap. Labonte emerged from the wreck with a broken shoulder, unable to drive.

This was bad news for Labonte, who was second in points but suddenly found himself unable to race. He would need a replacement driver who could compete against the most skilled stock car drivers in the country. That driver was Matt Kenseth. Labonte's crew chief, Jimmy Maker, had Kenseth waiting to take over from Labonte at the soonest possible opportunity so that the injured driver wouldn't have to run the whole race but would still be credited with points for participating in it. On the day of the race, Kenseth took over for Labonte after a rain delay.

Kenseth wouldn't be getting any points for his performance on the track. Any points he won would go to Labonte. The point of having a substitute driver is so that the primary driver doesn't fall too far behind in the standings, and

When Matt Kenseth substituted for an injured Bobby Labonte, seen here at Las Vegas Motor Speedway, he made NASCAR fans everywhere stand up and take notice.

any points are better than no points at all. It had been a good week for Kenseth—in fact, he'd won a Busch Series event over the weekend—and he managed to come in tenth place, earning 139 points for Labonte.

Joining Roush Racing

Roush Racing, one of the most prominent racing teams in NASCAR, saw the potential in Kenseth's tenacity. Team

Jack Roush, owner of Roush Racing, is sometimes called "The Cat in the Hat" due to his trademark Panama hat.

owner Jack Roush had been around race cars his entire life, building a powerful racing empire. The Roush team had a number of drivers in the Busch Series and the Winston Cup Series, including Mark Martin, a veteran driver who would become a mentor to Kenseth.

Martin liked Kenseth, whose style was not too different from his own. Although he's never won a championship, Martin is considered to be one of the best driver in NASCAR history. He never drives dirty or intentionally wrecks people. He is often referred to as "a racer's racer." Martin suggested that Roush take a chance on Kenseth.

In May 1999, DeWalt Tools signed a deal with Roush Racing. The sponsor wanted to field a Cup Series car driven by Kenseth, namely the #17 DeWalt Chevrolet. He

MARK MARTIN

Veteran racer Mark Martin is one of the best-loved drivers in NASCAR. Born in 1959, Martin established himself as a presence in the Cup Series in the early 1980s. He became a fan favorite and earned the nickname "Mr. Consistency." Martin has never won a championship, but he has been the season runner-up four times. In fact, at the end of each NASCAR season, more often than not, Martin is in the top ten in the final point standings.

Matt Kenseth makes no bones about the fact that he looks up to Martin and consciously patterns his driving style after his mentor's. Both racers are focused, determined, clean, and consistent. Martin is proud of his protégé's success. And, in a September 30, 1999, article in the Madison, Wisconsin, newspaper the *Capital Times*, Martin was quoted as saying, "[Kenseth] certainly turned out to be everything that I had hoped he would be and more . . . I saw that he had potential to be great, and I tried to make that happen. And in some small way, if he does something spectacular, I would feel the same success as if I had done it."

would run five races that year. For Kenseth, it was a dream come true. He was no longer just a substitute driver. Would his success in the Busch Series translate to the big leagues of the Cup Series? Interestingly enough, Kenseth's rival Dale Earnhardt Jr., who had triumphed over him to win two Busch Series championships, would also be getting a five-race Cup Series trial, with his father's team, Dale Earnhardt, Inc.

Trial Period

Kenseth's first Winston Cup race was at Michigan International Speedway in August 1999, where he finished a respectable 14th. The rest of the season proved to be a little more difficult. At Darlington, Kenseth crashed on the 145th lap. At Charlotte, another crash on the 231st lap resulted in a dismal 40th place finish. And in Rockingham, Kenseth's final Cup race of the year, engine trouble forced him out of the event.

But earlier in the year, on September 26, 1999, at Dover Downs International Speedway in Delaware, Kenseth finished fourth. He had been in the running to win but was pushed back into fourth place after a collision with Earnhardt Jr. It was an incredible finish for a newcomer who hadn't even had a full season of Cup Series racing under his belt yet. The winner of the race was veteran NASCAR driver Mark Martin, whom Kenseth would look to for advice and inspiration.

A Taste of Victory

Because he only ran five Cup Series races in 1999, Matt Kenseth would still be eligible for Rookie of the Year honors in 2000, when he would run a full 34 races. All eyes were on him, as well as on Earnhardt Jr.—his strongest competition for the Raybestos Rookie of the Year Award. Both were great drivers, and their rivalry was friendly, not personal.

Triumph at the Coca-Cola 600

Earnhardt Jr. won a race early in April and another race a month later, drawing the attention of the media and racing fans all over the country. But behind the scenes, Kenseth was driving solidly and racking up the points. On May 28, 2000, he became the first rookie ever to win the Coca-Cola 600 at Lowe's Motor Speedway in Concord, New Hampshire.

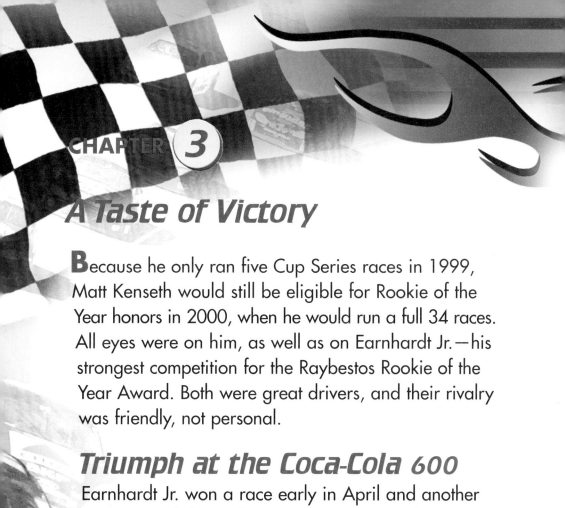

The Coca-Cola 600 is NASCAR's longest and toughest race. It demands all of a driver's endurance and focus. Starting in the 21st position, 28-year-old Kenseth worked his way through the pack, finally squeezing past Bobby Labonte to win by just over a half-second margin. Labonte finished second, followed by Dale Earnhardt Sr. in third and Dale Earnhardt Jr. in fourth.

In general, Kenseth does not wear his heart on his sleeve. He keeps his thoughts and feelings to himself and lets his driving speak for him. In fact, some of his detractors claim that he's boring. But Kenseth was ecstatic at his win and didn't hold back on the celebration. He tried to do doughnuts in the track infield like other drivers often do, but he was unable to pull it off—which no doubt amused those who admired Kenseth's consistency in every kind of difficult race condition. Having failed to execute doughnuts, he decided instead to do a reverse victory lap, which had been invented a decade before by fellow Wisconsin driver Alan Kulwicki. Even Kenseth's biggest rival was glad that he won. Earnhardt Jr. told reporters after the race, "I'm happy for him. He's a class act."

Rookie of the Year

By the end of the 2000 season, Kenseth came away with four top fives and 11 top-ten finishes. He consistently finished better than the other rookies in the field, ending the season 14th in points overall and with two million

Matt and Katie Kenseth pose for photos alongside the Winston Cup trophy, which Kenseth had won. The photo session in New York City was part of the 2003 Winston Cup Awards celebrations.

dollars in winnings. Best of all, he won the coveted Rookie of the Year Award.

It had been a huge year for Kenseth. He had success-fully raced against the country's best drivers in the Cup Series. He had risen to the top of the field to snag the Rookie of the Year Award. And on December 16, right before Christmas, he married his girlfriend, Katie Martin, who had also grown up in his hometown of Cambridge, Wisconsin. But most importantly, from a racing perspective, he had established himself in the Cup Series with a bang. The racing world waited with bated breath to see if Kenseth could turn his extraordinary early promise into NASCAR glory.

Triumph and Tragedy

With a supportive wife, a great mentor, and one of the best teams in racing behind him, Kenseth intended to finish the Winston Cup season in the top ten in 2001. He wasn't the only one on his team determined to be the best, however. His pit crew, led by crew chief Robbie Reiser, wowed the NASCAR world with their performance at the 2001 Unocal 76/Rockingham World Pit Crew Competition, where they set a world record for completing a full pit stop. During the season, they averaged pit stops under 15 seconds and were working to get their driver out of the pits and onto the track as fast as humanly

Although Matt Kenseth and Dale Earnhardt Jr. are NASCAR rivals, their competition ends when they get off the track. Here, the two young drivers talk in a Pocono Raceway garage.

possible. With a crew this good, all Kenseth had to do was drive fast and keep turning left.

However, the 2001 season began with heartbreak. During one of the final laps of the Daytona 500—the first and most popular race on the NASCAR calendar—the great Dale Earnhardt Sr. crashed headfirst into a wall. He died instantly. Needless to say, the NASCAR nation was stunned and saddened by the death of a true racing

KILLER BEES!

Matt Kenseth's pit crew is known as "the Killer Bees" because of their trademark yellow and black uniforms.

The Killer Bees know that every second counts. The faster the crew completes a pit stop, the faster they can get their car back out onto the racetrack. The Killer Bees aren't just mechanics; they're an athletic team that trains together and works constantly to perfect their technique. Every type of pit stop is choreographed, just like a football play. The Killer Bees videotape their practices and later analyze the tapes to find ways to operate in the pit more quickly and efficiently.

The Killer Bees' hard work has definitely paid off. After winning the 2002 World Pit Crew Championship, they wowed NASCAR fans by winning the 2003 Championship, beating their old record by almost an entire second.

In 2008, a big change occurred within the ranks of the Killer Bees. Reiser, who had been with Kenseth throughout his Cup Series racing career, stepped down as crew chief to take a management position within Roush Racing. He was replaced by Chip Bolin, who had been an engineer and car chief for the #17. Only time will tell whether Bolin will lead the Killer Bees to stinging defeat or sweet success.

legend. But no one mourned more than Earnhardt's son, Kenseth's friend and rival, Dale Earnhardt Jr. The death of Dale Sr. would result in NASCAR instituting a number of rule changes to make the sport safer.

Kenseth got off to a relatively slow start that year. For instance, he garnered a dismal 37th place finish at the 2001 Cracker Barrel Old Country Store 500 at the Atlanta Motor Speedway in Georgia. Engine trouble on the 273rd lap forced him out of the race. Things finally picked up on April 8, when he finished sixth in the Virginia 500 at Martinsville Speedway in Martinsville, Virginia. In general, it was a somewhat patchy season, with several crashes forcing him to leave races early. Although Kenseth didn't get any wins, he placed in the top five four times and in the top ten nine times, coming away with $2.5 million in earnings. Ultimately, he finished the season in 13th place, right behind Mark Martin.

Promising Results

The tide turned for Kenseth in 2002. Granted, the 30-year-old racer got off on the wrong foot with a crash at the Daytona 500. But his next race, the Subway 400 at North Carolina Speedway in Rockingham, North Carolina, was an entirely different proposition. There, he led the pack on 152 laps, cruising to a first place victory. In fact, victory was the name of the game that year: Kenseth earned a career-high five race victories. His pit crew

The confetti flies as Matt Kenseth celebrates a victory at Michigan International Speedway. Although he has a reputation for dull consistency, Kenseth likes to win as much as any other driver.

deserved some of the credit for his high win rate, as they were one of the fastest crews in the sport. Kenseth told reporters, "It's been an unbelievable year. I never thought we'd be in victory lane. It's hard enough to get here once, much less five times."

Ultimately, the season championship went to driver Tony Stewart. But besides five wins, Kenseth placed in the top five 11 times and in the top ten 19 times. He finished in eighth place overall. Finishing in the top ten was special for Kenseth, but he wanted to do even better—and 2003 would prove to be his year.

A Victorious Season

It all came together for Kenseth in 2003. Because of his quiet yet consistent driving style, his performance on the track can draw less notice than that of some of his peers. That was never more the case than in the 2003 season, when he stayed just outside the spotlight, piling up the points while others battled for wins. By March 9, he had taken the lead in points. It was a lead that he maintained for the rest of the year. At one point, Kenseth was winning the points race by a margin of 400 points!

In fact, Kenseth gained only one victory in 2003: the UAW-Daimler Chrysler 400 at Las Vegas Motor Speedway. Otherwise, he simply drove well without attracting too much attention—at least at first. Most fans were focused on young racing phenom Ryan Newman, who won eight races that season.

As the season drew to a close, it was clear that no one was going to be able to stop Kenseth. By the last race of the season, the Ford 400 at Homestead-Miami Speedway in Homestead, Florida, he was a lock for the championship. Engine trouble forced him out of the race after only 28 laps, meaning that he finished dead last. But it didn't matter: with 12 top-five finishes and 25 top-ten finishes, no one could hope to overcome his season point total. He had to wait for the race to finish before he could celebrate his winning of the Winston Cup.

Kenseth grew up watching the Daytona 500 on TV every February, when the snow still lay thick and deep in Wisconsin. He dreamed of one day driving in that race and becoming a NASCAR champion. Now, that dream had come true. It was not only Kenseth's first ever championship, but it was also the first championship for his team owner, Jack Roush. Roush had already spent 15 years as a NASCAR owner. Now, the youngster he had hired on Mark Martin's advice had given him his first Cup Series championship.

CHAPTER 4

The Road Ahead

After helping Kenseth win the championship, crew chief Reiser went right back to work. In fact, he was working in the team's shop at 5 AM the very next day. A new season was coming up, and the #17 team wasn't going to rest on their laurels.

Still, as the Winston Cup champion, Kenseth had a lot of celebrating to do. It seemed like everyone wanted a piece of the champ, including none other than the president of the United States, George W. Bush. Kenseth met with the president at the White House on December 2, 2003, where he presented the Commander-in-Chief with a leather NASCAR championship jacket. He also got to tour the Capitol Building in Washington, D.C. Kenseth then went all the way to New York, the city that never sleeps, for the NASCAR awards banquet. There, he received more than

Kenseth presents President Bush with a NASCAR jacket during a White House visit with a number of other NASCAR drivers, including Jimmie Johnson *(left)* and Dale Earnhardt Jr. *(right)*.

nine million dollars in season earnings. His grandfather would never have to buy him tires again.

But perhaps the warmest welcome awaited Kenseth back in his hometown of Cambridge, Wisconsin. When he returned home for Thanksgiving, he was greeted by banners and signs celebrating his big win. The town even held a parade in his honor. The citizens of Cambridge were overjoyed that their hometown hero had earned his place in history as a Winston Cup champion.

New Directions

Not everyone was thrilled with Kenseth's victory, however. While many regarded his driving style as a true example of racing excellence, others felt that Kenseth was a boring driver. The fact that he had only managed to get one win in his quest for points didn't sit right with some fans. And NASCAR officials didn't want to risk losing fans. So, for the 2004 season, NASCAR introduced a new points system that promised to keep fans on the edge of their seats until the very last race of the season.

The new points system was called the Chase for the Championship (known as the Chase for the Sprint Cup as of 2008). The new rules completely changed the way that races would be scored. After the first 26 races of the season, the 12 drivers (although it was originally just ten drivers) with the most points go on to compete against each other in the last ten races of the season. These ten races are known as the Chase, and they are sort of like the playoffs in team sports such as football or baseball. The 12 drivers in the Chase have their point tallies reset so that everyone has the same 5,000 points. At the end of the Chase, the driver with the most points is crowned champion.

Racers compete for the lead at the Kobalt Tools 500 at Atlanta Motor Speedway. Kenseth would finish this race in eighth place, earning 142 points.

The Chase was designed to put a greater emphasis on winning races. Each of the 12 drivers competing in it get ten points for each of their wins prior to the Chase. For instance, if a driver won four races during the regular season, then he or she would get a bonus of 40 points. The new system was supposed to ensure that no one would be able to amass so many points that he or she could clinch the championship before the season was over. Some fans even began calling the new Chase structure "The Matt Kenseth Rule."

Another big change in the NASCAR world came in 2004, when Winston stepped down as the sponsor of the Cup Series. It was replaced by Nextel, which was in turn replaced by Sprint, the company that sponsors the series at the time of this writing. Kenseth was the last person to ever win the Winston Cup.

On the Right Track

Both fans and critics looked to Kenseth to see if he could repeat his 2003 success in 2004. However, it was not to be. He had 16 top-ten finishes and two early-season wins. But things became patchier as the season wore on, and crashes and engine trouble cut several of his races short. Kenseth ultimately finished a solid seventh in the final points standings. The winner of the Nextel Cup that year was his Roush Racing teammate Kurt Busch.

However, Kenseth notably won the International Race of Champions (IROC). IROC, which operated from 1973 to 2006, was a racing series that pitted champions from several different racing worlds—like NASCAR, Indy Car, and Formula One—against each other. IROC drivers competed in identical stock cars, prepared by one common crew. IROC was designed to be a contest of pure driver skill. Kenseth's IROC victory helped to prove that he was one of the best drivers that American racing had ever seen.

The 2005 season started off not with a bang but with a whimper, when engine trouble forced Kenseth out of the Daytona 500 after only 34 laps. He had one win, 12 top-five finishes, and 17 top-ten finishes. He finished a very respectable seventh overall in the points standings for the second year in a row. It was a good year for Roush Racing. Five of the 12 drivers in the 2005 Chase— Greg Biffle, Kurt Busch, Carl Edwards, Matt Kenseth, and Mark Martin—drove for Roush.

Kenseth drove hard in 2006, scoring a win in Fontana during the second race of the season. He scored three other wins that season, at Dover, Michigan, and Bristol. He only crashed once and earned a place in the Chase for the Cup. After a strong performance in the Chase, he finished second overall in the points standing, with 15 top-five finishes and 21 top-ten finishes. It was his second-best season to date.

In 2007, Kenseth finished an overall fourth, with two wins, 13 top fives, and a remarkable 22 top tens. After a race in Martinsville, Virginia, he and teammate Carl Edwards got into what appeared to be an argument that nearly turned physical. The volatile Edwards was upset that Kenseth had bumped him during the race. Tempers can run high in NASCAR, as in any competitive sport, but fans don't generally get to see the conflicts between teammates. But Edwards angrily approached Kenseth during a televised interview, which meant that the cameras caught it all. The Edwards-Kenseth brouhaha surprised some NASCAR fans who were used to thinking of Kenseth as a quiet, laid-back, and clean driver.

Behind the Scenes

Kenseth might be a fierce competitor, but he's known as an easy-going guy off the track. He lives with his wife, Katie, in Lake Norman, North Carolina, the heart of NASCAR country. The Kenseths have one son, Ross. Matt enjoys listening to heavy metal—in fact, he named his cat "Lars," after the drummer of the veteran heavy metal band Metallica. Kenseth and Katie hang out together during the racing season. As he told the *Capital Times* in 2003, "We're almost like best friends. We'll sit in the motor home and watch TV, play video games, or do whatever on the weekend when we're stuck at the racetrack."

Despite his busy race schedule, Kenseth tries to visit home several times a year. His parents still live in Cambridge, Wisconsin. There, they help run the Matt

Fans watch Matt Kenseth drive the #17 DeWalt car through Times Square as part of NASCAR's Champions' Week celebrations in New York City.

Kenseth Fan Club Headquarters, where Kenseth fanatics can visit a Matt Kenseth Museum.

Even though he's a NASCAR champ, Kenseth hasn't let success change him. He's still a small-town guy from Wisconsin—who happens to be one of the greatest stock car drivers that the country has ever known. His victories have come through hard work, persistence, consistency, and concentration. His story proves that you don't need to be a superman to become a super racer. Sometimes, all you need to be the best is to do your best. And, once in a while, good guys actually finish first.

Glossary

conservative Moderate or cautious. Matt Kenseth is considered to be a conservative driver because he often does not run risks on the track.

crew chief The crew chief leads the pit crew and supervises the mechanics. It is an important position, as races can be won and lost in the pits. The crew chief is generally in contact with the driver via a microphone in the driver's helmet and makes many technical decisions during each race.

formidable Intimidating in strength; awe-inspiring.

mentor An important teacher and friend who guides his or her pupil.

moonshine Illegal, home-produced alcohol. Moonshine can be dangerous and even fatal to those who drink it.

pit crew The mechanics who maintain and repair race cars while the races are in progress. Seven members are allowed to attend to a car in NASCAR races.

Prohibition The period between 1920 and 1933 when the production, transport, sale, and consumption of alcohol were banned in the United States.

protégé A student trained by an experienced teacher.

qualifying lap In NASCAR, the starting order of the cars is determined by how well they do on a qualifying lap taken before the race.

rookie Someone who is new to something. In NASCAR, a rookie is a driver who is in his or her first season.

sponsor In NASCAR, racing teams are funded by a number of companies, or sponsors, which provide money in exchange for advertising. Matt Kenseth's main sponsor, whose logo is on the hood of his car and on his racing suit, is DeWalt Tools.

stock car The vehicles driven in NASCAR are stock cars. At one time, stock cars were closely related to the cars available to the general public.

For More Information

Matt Kenseth Fan Club
700 Kenseth Way
Cambridge, WI 53523
(866) 878-1717
Web site: http://www.mattkenseth.com/html/fanclub.html
Matt Kenseth's fan club includes a lot of Kenseth memorabilia and
    exhibits. It is open to visitors.

The NASCAR Foundation
One Wachovia Center
301 South College Street, Suite 3900
Charlotte, NC 28202
(704) 348-9682
Web site: http://foundation.nascar.com
The NASCAR Foundation supports a wide range of charitable initiatives
    that reflect the core values of the entire NASCAR family. The
    foundation uses the strength of the sport and its people to make
    a difference in the lives of those who need it most.

National Association for Stock Car Auto Racing (NASCAR)
P.O. Box 2875
Daytona Beach, FL 32120
Web site: http://www.nascar.com
(866) 722-5299
NASCAR is the sanctioning body for one of North America's premier
    sports. NASCAR is the number one spectator sport in the United
    States and is the number two–rated regular season sport on tele-
    vision. It consists of three national series (the NASCAR Sprint Cup
    Series, NASCAR Nationwide Series, and NASCAR Craftsman
    Truck Series), four regional series, and one local grassroots series,
    as well as two international series. NASCAR sanctions more than
    1,200 races at 100 tracks in more than 30 U.S. states, Canada,
    and Mexico.

For More Information

Roush Automotive Collection
11851 Market Street
Livonia, MI 48150
(734) 779-7290
Web site: http://www.roushcollection.com
This collection features cars and other memorabilia from Roush Racing.

Roush Fenway Racing Museum
4600 Roush Place NW
Concord, NC 28027
(704) 720-4350
Web site: http://www.roushfenwaycorporate.com/Museum/default.asp
This museum created by Roush Fenway Racing, one of the leading
    NASCAR racing teams, includes historic race cars from the drag
    racing past up to the NASCAR present.

Winston Cup Museum
1355 North Martin Luther King Jr. Drive
Winston-Salem, NC 27101
(336) 724-4557
Web site: http://www.winstoncupmuseum.com
This museum is dedicated to the 33-year history of Winston Cup racing.
    Matt Kenseth was the final winner of the Winston Cup before it
    was renamed the Nextel and then the Sprint Cup.

Web Sites

Due to the changing nature of Internet links, Rosen Publishing has
developed an online list of Web sites related to the subject of this book.
This site is updated regularly. Please use this link to access this list:

http://www.rosenlinks.com/bw/kens

For Further Reading

Armentrout, David, and Patricia Armentrout. *Matt Kenseth: In the Fast Lane.* Vero Beach, FL: Rourke Publishing, 2007.

Barber, Phil. *From Finish to Start: A Week in the Life of a NASCAR Racing Team.* Maple Plain, MN: Tradition Books, 2004.

Buckley, James. *NASCAR.* New York, NY: DK Children, 2005.

Burt, William. *NASCAR's Best: Top Drivers Past and Present.* Osceola, WI: Motorbooks, 2004.

Dallenbach, Robin, and Anita Rich. *Portraits of NASCAR.* Marietta, GA: Motorsports Family LLC, 2008.

Gabbard, Alex. *NASCAR's Wild Years: Stock-Car Technology in the 1960s.* North Branch, MN: CarTech, Inc., 2005.

Martin, Mark, and Beth Tuschak. *NASCAR for Dummies.* Hoboken, NJ: Wiley Publishing, Inc., 2005.

Maruszweski, Kelley. *Matt Kenseth: Above and Beyond.* Champaign, IL: Sports Publishing LLC, 2003.

Robinson, Tom. *Mark Martin: Master Behind the Wheel* (Heroes of Racing). Berkeley Heights, NJ: Enslow Publishers, 2008.

Bibliography

Associated Press. "Pointed Comments: Kenseth Defends Current Scoring System." *Capital Times*, August 19, 2003: 4D.

Buckley, Tim. "Kenseth's Success Fuels Much Interest." *St. Petersburg Times*, April 1, 1999: 3C.

Capital Times. "NASCAR Noticing Kenseth: Martin Guiding Cambridge Native." September 30, 1999: 1C.

Capital Times. "Reiser Signs Kenseth for Rest of Season." May 2, 1997: 1B.

Engh, Brent. "Cambridge Crazy for Kenseth." *Capital Times*, August 19, 1999: 7C.

Fryer, Jenna. "Vanilla and Victorious: Cambridge's Matt Kenseth Quietly Sits on Top of the Standings on NASCAR's Premier Circuit." *Wisconsin State Journal*, April 18, 2003: C1.

Harris, Mike. "Kenseth Visits White House: Bush Honors Winston Cup Champion, NASCAR Stars." *Capital Times*, December 3, 2003: 1D.

Jenkins, Chris. "Kenseth Learned to Steer Clear of Crashes by Starting from Back." *USA Today*, December 3, 2003: C02.

Jenkins, Chris. "Title Path Wasn't Smooth Emotionally." *USA Today*, November 18, 2003: 4E.

Kelley, Kevin. "'Other Rookie' Kenseth Triumphs." *St. Petersburg Times*, May 29, 2000: 1C.

Livinston, Seth. "How the Chase Was Won." *USA Today*, November 22, 2006: 4E.

Minter, Rick. "What's the Point? Points Leader Matt Kenseth and Contender Jeff Gordon Ponder Why NASCAR Rewards Consistency Over Winning." *Wisconsin State Journal*, July 26, 2003: C1.

Newton, David. "Not All Teammates Cut in the Mold of Jeff Gordon and Jimmie Johnson." ESPN.com, October 27, 2007. Retrieved April 2008 (http://sports.espn.go.com/rpm/columns/story?seriesId=2&id=3082116).

Schnatz, Pete. "Kenseth Savoring Victory Lap." *Philadelphia Inquirer*, December 3, 2003: E02.

MATT KENSETH: NASCAR Driver

Sferazo, Stephen. "Getting to Know Matt Kenseth." SpeedwayMedia. com, July 25, 2006. Retrieved April 2008 (http://www. speedwaymedia.com/Articles/06/072506Sferazo.asp).

Sheldon, Kathy. "Stinging Sensation: Matt Kenseth's Pit Crew Has Been the Best Two Years Running. Now, the Killer Bees and Kenseth Are Flying Toward a Winston Cup Championship." *Sporting News*, July 28, 2003. Retrieved April 2008 (http://findarticles.com/ p/articles/mi_m1208/is_30_227/ai_105915641).

Smith, Marty. "Conversation: Matt Kenseth." NASCAR.com, December 2, 2003. Retrieved April 2008 (http://www. nascar.com/2003/news/features/conversation/12/03/ mkenseth_conversation/index.html).

St. Petersburg Times. "Kenseth Is Basking in Title Glow." December 5, 2003: 3C.

Surprenant, Tamira. "Wife in the Fast Lane: Katie Kenseth Plays Key Role in Matt's Success." *Capital Times*, August 18, 2003: 1D.

Voda, Krista. "Behind the Chase: Kenseth's More Than a 'Pretty Woman.'" FOXSports.com, September 27, 2005. Retrieved April 2008 (http://msn.foxsports.com/nascar/story/4910568/ Behind-the-Chase:-Kenseth's-more-than-a-'Pretty-Woman').

Wisconsin State Journal. "Parents Cheer from Home: Although Not Able to Attend the Coca-Cola 600 in Person, Roy and Nicki Kenseth Rejoice in their Son's Victory." May 29, 2000: 6C.

Index

A

American Speed Association (ASA), 12

C

Chase for the Sprint Cup, 35, 37, 38

D

Dale Earnhardt, Inc., 22
DeWalt Tools, 17, 20

E

Earnhardt racing dynasty, 13

F

Formula One racing, 6, 38

I

Indy Car racing, 6, 38
International Race of Champions (IROC), 38

K

Kenseth, Matt
  driving style, 16–17, 20, 24, 35
  early years, 8–13, 34
  in the media, 21, 24, 31, 39
  mentor of, 20–21, 22, 29, 32
  as NASCAR champ, 7, 23–24, 26–27, 29, 31–35, 37–40
  pit crew of, 26–27, 28, 29, 31
  private life of, 26, 39–40
  pro racing start, 11–20, 22
  racing setbacks, 4, 29, 32, 37
  reputation of, 5–6, 7, 39, 40
  as Rookie of the Year, 24, 26
  sponsors of, 17, 20
  trip to White House, 33
Killer Bees pit crew, 28

M

Martin, Mark, 20–21, 22, 29, 32
Matt Kenseth Fan Club, 40
Matt Kenseth Museum, 40
"Matt Kenseth Rule," 37

N

NASCAR, history of, 6–7
NASCAR series
  Busch, 11–13, 17, 18, 19, 20, 22
  Coca-Cola 600, 23–24
  Daytona 500, 27, 29, 32, 38
  Sprint/Nextel Cup, 14, 35, 37
  Winston Cup, 4, 14–15, 18, 20, 22, 26, 32, 33, 35, 37

R

Reiser, Robbie, 12, 17, 26, 28, 33
Roush, Jack, 20, 32
Roush Racing, 19–20, 28, 37, 38

About the Author

Jeffrey Spaulding is a writer and editor living in New York State. He was first introduced to NASCAR by his older brother and remains a fan to this day.

Photo Credits

Cover, pp. 1, 4, 5, 8, 14, 15, 17, 19, 20, 23, 25, 27, 30, 33, 34, 36, 40 © Getty Images, p. 10 © AP Photos.

Designer: Evelyn Horovicz; Photo Researcher: Marty Levick